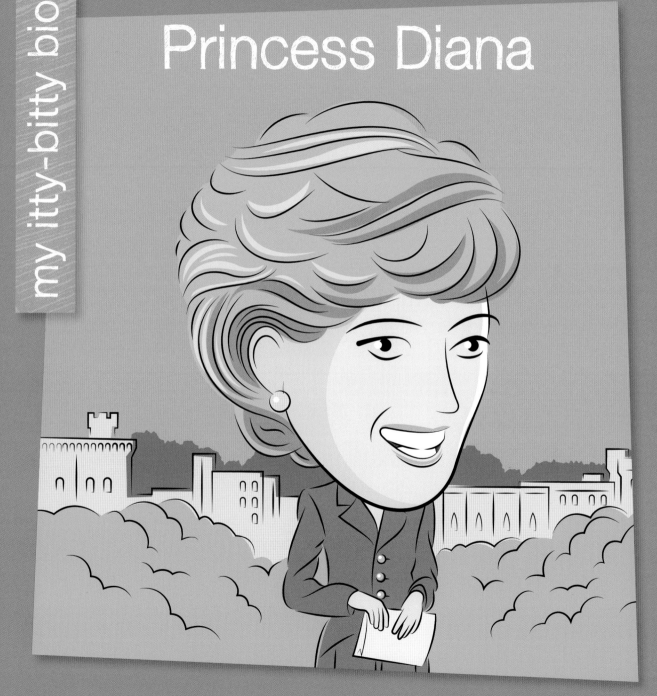

Princess Diana

Published in the United States of America by Cherry Lake Publishing Group
Ann Arbor, Michigan
www.cherrylakepublishing.com

Reading Adviser: Marla Conn, MS Ed., Literacy specialist, Read-Ability, Inc.
Book Designer: Jennifer Wahi
Illustrator: Jeff Bane

Photo Credits: ©Jim Linwood/flickr, 5; ©LightField Studios/shutterstock, 7; ©Joe Haupt/flickr, 9, 11, 17, 22; ©rook76/shutterstock, 13, 23; ©Russ Quinlan/flickr, 15; ©Tim Graham/Uploaded by Uncoveringcelebrityhistory/Wikimedia, 19; ©Public Domain/Robert Sullivan/flickr, 21; Jeff Bane, Cover, 1, 6, 10, 16

Cherry Lake Press is an imprint of Cherry Lake Publishing Group.

Library of Congress Cataloging-in-Publication Data

Names: Pincus, Meeg, author. | Bane, Jeff, 1957- illustrator.
Title: Princess Diana / Meeg Pincus ; illustrated by , Jeff Bane.
Description: Ann Arbor, Michigan : Cherry Lake Publishing, 2021. | Series:
   My itty-bitty bio | Includes index. | Audience: Grades K-1 | Summary:
   "The My Itty-Bitty Bio series are biographies for the earliest readers.
   This book examines the life and legacy of Princess Diana, mother of
   Prince William and Prince Harry, in a simple, age-appropriate way that
   will help young readers develop word recognition and reading skills.
   Includes a table of contents, author biography, timeline, glossary,
   index, and other informative backmatter"-- Provided by publisher.
Identifiers: LCCN 2020035872 (print) | LCCN 2020035873 (ebook) | ISBN
   9781534179967 (hardcover) | ISBN 9781534181670 (paperback) | ISBN
   9781534180970 (pdf) | ISBN 9781534182684 (ebook)
Subjects: LCSH: Diana, Princess of Wales, 1961-1997--Juvenile literature. |
   Princesses--Great Britain--Biography--Juvenile literature.
Classification: LCC DA591.A45 P56 2021 (print) | LCC DA591.A45 (ebook) |
   DDC 941.085092 [B]--dc23
LC record available at https://lccn.loc.gov/2020035872
LC ebook record available at https://lccn.loc.gov/2020035873

Printed in the United States of America
Corporate Graphics

table of contents

About the author: Meeg Pincus has been a writer, editor, and educator for 25 years. She loves to write inspiring stories for kids about people, animals, and our planet. She lives near San Diego, California, where she enjoys the beach, reading, singing, and her family.

About the illustrator: Jeff Bane and his two business partners own a studio along the American River in Folsom, California, home of the 1849 Gold Rush. When Jeff's not sketching or illustrating for clients, he's either swimming or kayaking in the river to relax.

I was born in England. It was 1961. I had three **siblings**.

5

I loved music and dancing.
I worked with children.

I married Prince Charles.
I became a princess. My wedding was on television. People around the world watched. My dress had 10,000 pearls!

I traveled to many countries.
People **admired** me. I was a
role model.

What do you admire in others?

I had two sons, Prince William and Prince Harry. I loved being a mother.

35c
OSTAGE

NEW
ZEALAND
1985

13

I did **charity** work. I helped the sick and the **homeless**. I helped countries after wars.

Where would you like to help?

Most **royals** did not talk about feelings. But I did. I was unhappy. I talked about my struggles. I wanted people to know they weren't alone.

I was called the "People's Princess." I was most proud of my children and my charity work.

I died in a car crash. It was 1997. I was only 36. People around the world were shocked and sad. But my legacy lives on. I am remembered for my kindness and warmth.

What would you like to ask me?

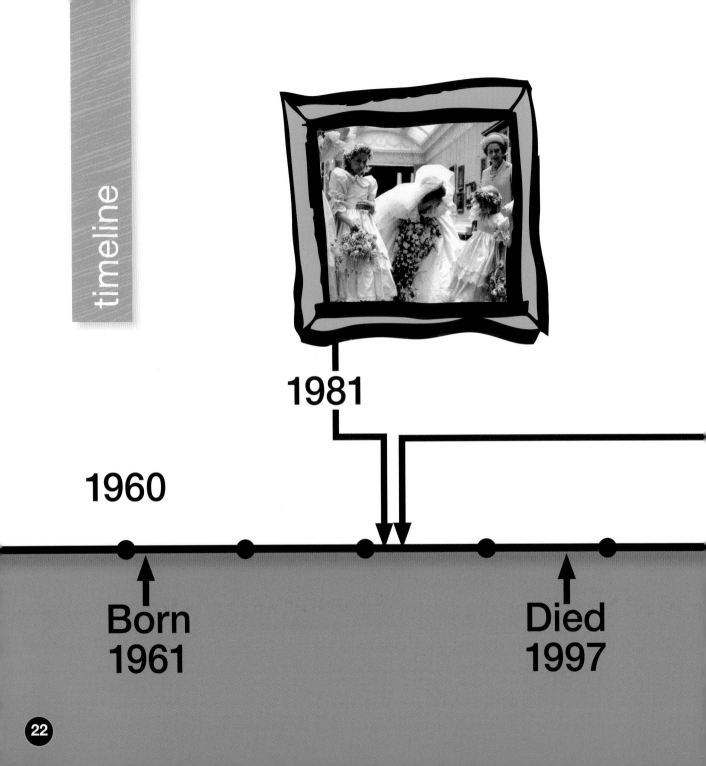

1981

1960

Born
1961

Died
1997

1982

2060

glossary

admired (ad-MIRED) thought very highly of

charity (CHAR-ih-tee) money or other help given to people in need

homeless (HOME-lis) people without a permanent home or place to sleep

role model (ROHL MAH-duhl) a person who people look up to

royals (ROI-uhlz) members of the family of the queen or king

siblings (SIB-lingz) brothers and sisters

index